BRUCE & STAN'S®

POCKET GUIDE TO

KNOWING God's Will

BRUCE BICKEL and STAN JANTZ

HARVEST HOUSE PUBLISHERS
Eugene, Oregon 97402

Scripture quotations are taken from the *Holy Bible*, New Living Translation, copyright © 1996. Used by permission of Tyndale House Publishers, Inc., Wheaton, Illinois 60189, USA. All rights reserved.

Cover by Left Coast Design, Portland, Oregon

Cover illustration by Krieg Barrie Illustrations, Hoquiam, Washington

BRUCE & STAN'S® POCKET GUIDE TO KNOWING GOD'S WILL
Copyright © 2002 by Bruce Bickel and Stan Jantz
Published by Harvest House Publishers
Eugene, Oregon 97402

Library of Congress Cataloging-in-Publication Data
  ISBN 0-7369-0756-4 (pbk.)

Printed in the United States of America.

02 03 04 05 06 07 08 09 10 / BP-CF / 10 9 8 7 6 5 4 3 2 1

Contents

A Note from the Authors

Pity the poor people who have no faith in God. When they want to know the answers for their future, they are stuck with sources like the horoscope on the comics page of the newspaper. Or, if they have a credit card, they can talk to a phony phone psychic for $19.95 for three minutes. Or, if they are really desperate, they can consult the Magic Eight Ball. Whatever their decision, they are taking a stab in the dark. Without clear direction, we naturally worry about the decisions we made in the past and fret about the decisions we have yet to make about our future.

But those of us who believe in God know the One who knows the future. We can go directly to Him for advice when we have big (or small) decisions to make. There is no better source for direction in our lives than God Himself. After all, since He knows everything and wants what is best for us, all we have to do is find "His will" for any decision that confronts us. Nothing could be simpler. Ask God to reveal His perfect plan, and then do it. All of life's major decisions suddenly become simple.

No doubting. No second-guessing. And everything turns out perfectly.

Yeah, right. Unfortunately, finding God's will is a lot more frustrating for most people than using the Magic Eight Ball. You can't ask God a question, then shake Him, turn Him upside down, and find your printed answer. At times you might even feel that God is keeping His plan hidden despite your desperate pleas for Him to reveal it.

This Book Is for You If...

If you didn't care about God, you wouldn't be reading this book. But you do, so you are. Your love for God makes you want to do His will. So, why does He make His will so difficult to figure out?

This book is designed to give you some plain and simple principles for finding God's will. If you are like us, then you're more interested in knowing God's plan itself than the theology of it. You want to know about God's will because you have some decisions that need to be made, not because you are preparing for an essay exam in a seminary class. This book is for you if...

- You are eager to follow God's plan for your life, but you have no idea what it is.

- You are approaching a deadline on making some major decisions in your life, and you want God to give you some sort of "sign" to guide you. (Celestial skywriting would be nice. Nothing fancy. Something in a New Times Roman font would be sufficient.)

- You are jealous of all of your other Christian friends who seem to know exactly what God wants them to do with their lives. They seem to be focused and directed, but you're still wandering around aimlessly. You are particularly envious of those Christians who "heard God's call." You never heard a call. You are starting to take shorter showers because you don't want to miss one if it comes.

- You are freaking out over some impending life-changing decision such as where to go to college, who to marry, or what career to pursue.

You've been praying for so long without an answer that you are beginning to resent God for making His choice so difficult to determine.

- It's not the big problems in life that bother you; it's the small ones. Because God knows the number of hairs on your head, you're wondering if He has a perfect will for how you should cut your hair.

- Your anxiety over finding God's will is ruining your enjoyment of God's love.

- You followed God's direction in the past, but now things aren't going so well. You are beginning to wonder whether you got God's signals correct in the first place. Maybe you zigged when He really wanted you to zag. Can you ever get back on track, or are you destined to live in Plan B for the rest of your existence?

If You Are Looking for Signs Along the Way...

God isn't likely to put road signs along your morning commute route that reveal

His will. So you probably won't see a billboard that says: "I've heard your prayers. The answers are *yes* to the job change, *wait* on the marriage proposal, and buy the *midnight blue* Accord. Love, God." But we know you're anxious for some definite guidance in your life, so we've put a few icons in the margins of this book.

Big Idea—This icon saves you the trouble of marking the sentence with a yellow highlighter. It's that important.

Key Verse—Every verse from the Bible is significant, but this icon identifies the ones that are worth re-reading before you move on down the page.

It's a Mystery—We don't know everything about God, but we don't feel bad about it. Nobody does. At least we admit it.

Glad You Asked—You aren't alone when it comes to wondering how to find God's will. We can anticipate some of your questions because we've asked them ourselves.

Learn the Lingo—We try to stay away from terminology that is used more often in the monastery than in the mall. Occasionally we can't help ourselves.

Dig Deeper—This book is just a "pocket guide" to the subject of God's will. In case you want to study this fascinating subject in greater detail, we'll give you the titles of some good books.

We've Got Good News for You!

Your life is going to be energized in a new way when you discover how to live within God's will. You'll be able to face tough decisions with confidence. You'll have a sense of assurance as you navigate through the choices in life. But don't take our word for it. Look at what God says about it:

> *"For I know the plans I have for you," says the Lord. "They are plans for good and not for disaster, to give you a future and a hope"* (Jeremiah 29:11).

God has a plan for your life, and you are probably very anxious to learn all about it. Well, we've got good news for you. The process of discovering God's will for your life may not be as complicated as you think.

Chapter 1

God Is Large and in Charge

> *History is the record of divine manifestations imperfectly understood.*
>
> —Leopold von Ranke

BRUCE & STAN SAY

No one cares about finding "Bruce's will" or knowing "Stan's plan." And rightly so. Our track record reveals that we don't know much about the future. (Investing our entire 401(k) accounts in stock of Pets.com was proof of that.) Even if we were wise enough to know a little about the future, we still wouldn't be able to influence or change it very much.

There wouldn't be much sense in finding *God's will* either if He didn't know about the future or couldn't do anything about it. But unlike us, God does and He can.

In this first chapter we are going to review the nature and character traits of God. We think that you will be impressed with how much God knows about you and how much He is involved in the events of your life. That information may make you even more curious about His plan for your life.

Bruce & Stan

Chapter 1

God Is Large and in Charge

*O*ur favorite part of eating Chinese food happens after the meal is over. Sure, some of the gastronomic delicacies are delicious, but the real thrill of Chinese dining comes when the dishes are cleared and everyone grabs for one of those shrink-wrapped fortune cookies. You know what we are talking about. There is a ceremony at the end of dinner when everyone cracks open his or her cookie. Few people actually eat the cookie (which has the flavor of a stale vanilla wafer and the consistency of an egg carton), but everyone takes a turn reading aloud his or her "fortune." Every strip of paper has a different message, but they usually center on a theme such as: "Prosperity is headed your way if you show generosity to others." (It makes you wonder if the waiters themselves compose these sayings in an attempt to obtain bigger tips.)

There is something very interesting about Chinese fortune cookies. Everybody likes to read the "fortune," but nobody takes it seriously. It is not surprising that these wise-sounding prognostications are ignored. After all, they are written by some guy who:

✓ Has no idea who you are...

✓ Lacks any reliable insight into the future

✓ Can't be trusted to help you have a successful life (since his own bleak existence consists of sitting in some windowless room for 18 hours a day cranking out 1,500 fortunes on his titanium G4 Powerbook)

People don't laminate their fortunes to carry in their wallets. Those strips of paper are either wadded into a ball or used to dislodge chow mein that is stuck between your teeth. You aren't going to change your life based on that Chinese fortune cookie because you have no reason to believe its message.

By now you are probably wondering what Chinese fortune cookies have to do with finding the will of God. We don't blame you for wondering, but we are about to make an analogy between them. Actually, we think you'll be surprised at how profound our analogy is. (We surprised ourselves because it doesn't happen very often.) Here it is:

Unless you believe that God's plan for your life is reliable and relevant, it will be as meaningless to you as that fortune cookie.

Why Are You Looking for God's Will?

Before we explore the reliability and relevance of God's will, allow us to ask you *why* you are trying to find it. Your motivation might be due to:

✓ *Reverence:* You have put God in control of your life. Doing whatever God says

and going wherever He directs you
seems like the religious thing to do.

✓ *Curiosity:* You want to call your own
shots in life, but it would be helpful if
you had a few clues about your future.

✓ *Confusion:* You are currently faced with
some tough issues in your life. You
need God's help to make a decision.
Once He gets you past this rough spot,
you'll take it from there.

✓ *Desperation:* You've made a mess of
things so far. God is your last resort
for help.

Why do we bother asking about your motivation for seeking God's will? Well, your
motivation may profoundly influence the
way you respond to God's will when you
find it. Here we go getting profound again:

Your desire to know and follow
God's will is directly proportional to your belief that He
knows what is best for you and is
able to do something about it.

If you are just mildly curious about God's
will, or if you are only interested in it as a
quick fix to get you out of a problem, then

God won't have much more credibility for you than the fortune cookie writer. That perception of God (and your response to His will) is bound to change if you become convinced that God's will is relevant to your life and that it is entirely reliable.

In the sections that follow we will be reviewing the biblical foundation for why God is more trustworthy than a Chinese fortune cookie. As you will see, He knows all about you and your future, and He is intimately and actively involved in the details of your life. Finding and following God's will for your life makes sense because of who He is, what He knows, and what He wants to do for you.

God Has What It Takes

When it comes to choosing your advisors, your options are rather bleak:

- ✓ Most of the people you know aren't much smarter than you are. They might be willing to offer you some advice, but you might do better on your own.

- ✓ Except for a few family members or friends, other people are more interested in their own welfare than in yours. Can you really trust their advice? (We've got three words for you: used car salesman.)

✓ You have to worry about the hype. Whether you are considering an investment, a career, or a move to another city, your decision is complicated by separating the truth from the propaganda. Is it too good to be true? How can you know for sure?

As you consider the plans for your life, wouldn't you prefer to go to an all-knowing source...someone like the Wizard of Oz? Well, God is everything that you need (and you won't be disappointed by finding some guy hiding behind a curtain).

We don't know what you think about God. Maybe you feel that He is like a blind date—you don't know what He looks like, but you have been told that He has a great personality. He does have a great personality. And with respect to finding God's will, those character traits (called *attributes*) are everything that you would want from someone who was going to help you plan your life.

God Is Omniscient

God knows everything. All things past and all things future. He knows all things technical (like the chemical composition of DNA) and all things trivial (like the number of hairs on your head, which may not be trivial to a guy with a receding hairline). He knows you better than you know yourself.

> *O Lord, you have examined my heart and know everything about me. You know when I sit down or stand up. You know my every thought when far away. You chart the path ahead of me and tell me where to stop and rest. Every moment you know where I am. You know what I am going to say even before I say it, Lord* (Psalm 139:1-4).

If you are going to be looking to someone to guide you through life, this omniscience trait could prove to be very useful. Because God has all knowledge, His judgments are always made wisely. He sees all things in their proper perspective, and He is never surprised by new information that would require a change in His plans.

God Is Omnipresent

He is everywhere, all at the same time. This means that you can't escape or hide from Him no matter how hard you try. But it also means that He is always with you no matter where you are.

> *I can never escape from your spirit! I can never get away from your presence! If I go up to heaven, you are there; if I go down to the place of the dead, you are there. If I ride the wings of the morning, if I dwell by the farthest oceans, even there your hand will guide me, and your strength will support me. I could ask the darkness to hide me and the light around me to become night—but even in darkness I cannot hide from you. To you the night shines as bright as day. Darkness and light are both alike to you* (Psalm 139:7-12).

Even if you have made poor decisions that have taken you down the wrong road in life, you can never get beyond God's presence.

God Is Omnipotent

He is all-powerful. No person, nation, or confederation, whether of this earth or beyond, can conquer Him. He is able to do anything consistent with His own nature.

> *O Sovereign Lord! You have made the heavens and earth by your great power. Nothing is too hard for you* (Jeremiah 32:17).

This aspect of God's nature is not limited to phenomena such as creating the world, navigating plagues of locusts, or walking on water. Amazingly, this power also affects human events. So don't abandon hope in God's plan just because someone is standing in the way; God can work effectively to change circumstances, whether your own or others'.

The extent of God's attributes is not exhausted with these three *omni* words. He has several other personality traits that make Him the perfect One to be in charge of your life planning. For example:

God Is Just

He is fair and impartial. He does not play favorites.

> *He is the Rock; his work is perfect. Everything he does is just and fair* (Deuteronomy 32:4).

There will be times when life seems unfair. If you are operating under God's plan, however, you can be assured that He is dealing equitably with you because that is the essence of His nature.

God Is Holy

He is righteous. No fault is found in Him. His moral character is without flaw. There is not a bit of evil in Him; He is completely pure. In other words, He is wholly holy.

> *In a great chorus they sang, "Holy, holy, holy is the Lord Almighty! The whole earth is filled with his glory"* (Isaiah 6:3).

God's direction will never lead you down the wrong path. He can't go there Himself, and it is against His nature to direct you in error.

God Is Love

God's love is not a romantic feeling (as Hollywood usually defines *love*). In contrast, God's love refers to unselfishness and commitment. He is ready to forgive and desires to be merciful toward you.

> *Dear friends, let us continue to love one another, for love comes from God. Anyone*

*who loves is born of God and knows God.
But anyone who does not love does not
know God—for God is love. God showed
how much he loved us by sending his only
Son into the world so that we might have
eternal life through him. This is real love.
It is not that we love God, but that he
loved us and sent his Son as a sacrifice to
take away our sins* (1 John 4:7-10).

Because God loves you, He won't sabotage
your life with some fiendish scheme because
He is holding a grudge against you. God
loves you and wants what is best for you.

God Is Immutable

God doesn't change. His character is
always the same—yesterday, today, and
tomorrow.

> *I am the Lord, and I do not change*
> (Malachi 3:6).

There are a lot of things that change
unexpectedly and throw your life into tur-
moil, such as income tax changes, airline
schedules, and your spouse's moods. But
you'll never be surprised or disappointed
with God's attitudes. You can plan your life
around them.

Life is tough if you have to make all of your decisions by yourself. First, you've got to know the right thing to do. Then, you must have the will to do it. (Even if we know what needs to be done, we may lack the desire.) Finally, we need the ability to accomplish it. With God's attributes, however, He is never frustrated over what to do:

- ✓ He is wise, so He always knows what to do.

- ✓ He is good, so He always chooses to do the right thing.

- ✓ He is powerful, and therefore, always capable of doing what He wills to do.

If you are seeking advice and direction in life, aren't those the kind of character qualities you are looking for?

God Is Running the Show

Imagine the Apostle Paul and Charles Darwin arguing with each other on one of those cable television shows. (Not a Jerry Springer-type show. One of those news-type shows where there is still a lot of yelling but the panelists are dressed in business suits instead of overalls or spandex tube tops.) Their conversation might go something like this:

Darwin: There is no order in the universe. It is spinning randomly in space. Things just happen. There is no reason to it all.

Paul: Hold on a minute, Chuck. God created the universe, and He is still in control of all that is happening in the world.

Darwin: God? There is no god who created the world. And even if there is, he is nothing more than an absentee landlord who no longer has anything to do with his property. I'm so sure of that fact, I'd stake my life on it.

Paul: I'm sorry to hear that.

In contradiction to Darwin's position, the Bible describes God as being *sovereign*. That means everything happens according to His will and plan. The Bible doesn't beat around a burning bush on this point. It boldly and repeatedly declares that God is totally and completely in charge of everything.

> *The Lord does whatever pleases him through-*
> *out all heaven and earth (Psalm 135:6).*

God's sovereignty covers everything:

- From the big, cataclysmic occurrences in the universe (Revelation 4:11), to the miniscule details of your life (James 4:13-15)

- From international politics (Proverbs 21:1), to your physical, emotional, and psychological problems (1 Peter 3:17)

There is nothing in all of creation that is outside of God's sovereign control. (Since God created everything, it makes sense that He continues to control all of it.) Proverbs 16:33 even says that God determines the roll of the dice. (Caution: Don't interpret this verse as a biblical mandate for gambling in Las Vegas. It says the Lord determines how the dice will fall, but it doesn't say He will make them fall in your favor.)

The sovereignty of God means that nothing happens in the universe—or in our lives—without God allowing it. Because He is sovereign, God is better at designing a plan for your life than you are. Think about it:

- Nothing ever catches God by surprise, it happens only if He allows it.

- There is nothing that He can't handle; everything is under His control.

- He doesn't worry about what will happen next.

- He always has the correct response to the events that occur.

You probably can't say those things about yourself, so aren't you glad you've got Someone on your side who is sovereign?

WHAT IF YOU CAN'T MAKE SENSE OF IT ALL?

Because God is omniscient, holy, and righteous—and you aren't—you are in no position to judge God for what He does and what He allows. You need to trust His judgment instead of your own when His sovereignty allows events in your life that you don't understand.

Jesus told a parable about people who object to certain details of God's sovereign plan. The story is about a master who hired some workers early in the morning; as the day went on, he kept hiring more. By the end of the day, some workers had labored all day, others had worked about half a day, and some had only worked for an hour or two. But the master paid them all the same amount that he promised to those who began work at the beginning of the day. The men who put in the most hours started to complain about the apparent injustice of the wage scale. The boss cut them off with the following statement:

> *Friend, I haven't been unfair! Didn't you agree to work all day for the usual wage? Take it and go. I wanted to pay this last worker the same as you. Is it against the law for me to do what I want with my money? Should you be angry because I am kind?* (Matthew 20:13-15).

The Apostle Paul also pointed out that it is ridiculous for us to question God's wisdom.

> *Who are you, a mere human being, to criticize God? Should the thing that was created say to the one who made it, "Why have you made me like this?" When a potter makes jars out of clay, doesn't he have a right to use the same lump of clay to make one jar for decoration and another to throw garbage into? God has every right to exercise his judgment and his power...* (Romans 9:20-23).

God's sovereignty isn't something that should bother you. Just the contrary. Although you might not understand (or even like) what is happening, you can rest in the assurance that God knows what He is doing and has everything under control.

Providence Is Not Just a City in Rhode Island

It's time for a little review. So far we have discussed that:

- God is large (all of those omni attributes of God)

- God is in charge (His sovereignty)

But an accurate understanding of how God operates in the world gets a little more complicated because of one thing: *you*. You are a key player in the world (in your own life at least), so any discussion about God being in charge of the world has to deal with how you fit into the picture.

Have you ever stopped to wonder how God interacts with humanity? Sure, He is large and in charge, but how involved is He in the day-to-day circumstances of your life? Does He pay attention to every little detail? Shouldn't the hole in the ozone layer and global warming involve more of His concentration than helping you decide which parking space to choose? Do you even want God to know about your facial blemishes when there are earthquakes and mudslides in Central America that need His attention?

Let's get even more personal. Beyond what God *knows* about you, how much does He get *involved* with the circumstances of your life? And do you consider His involvement to be a legitimate interest or an overbearing intrusion? Where does God's control stop and your personal freedom begin? Does one infringe on the other?

All of these questions relate to God's *providence*. Theologians use that term to describe God's continuing involvement in the daily events of the world (in general) and in your life (in particular) to bring about His intended results. God is not like some absentee landlord who never bothers to know what is going on with his property. God is not just a spectator-creator who brought you into this life and then left you to fend for yourself in the cold, cruel world with nothing but your own resources. (On the other hand, God is not some micro-manager who manipulates every single event of your life so that you have no choice and are like a pawn in a celestial chess game. We'll explore your ability to make your own choices in Chapter 2.)

God's Providence Means Our Preservation

There is a preservation aspect to God's providence. This involves protection and providing for needs:

✓ God's preservation applies to creation as a whole.

> *You alone are the Lord. You made the skies and the heavens and all the stars. You made the earth and the seas and everything in them. You preserve and give life to everything, and all the angels of heaven worship you* (Nehemiah 9:6).

✓ God's providence preserved the Israelites in the wilderness, by providing them with manna, quail, and water.

✓ Jesus assured the disciples that they didn't need to worry about food or clothing because God handles that.

> *So I tell you, don't worry about everyday life—whether you have enough food,*

drink, and clothes. Doesn't life consist of more than food and clothing? Look at the birds. They don't need to plant or harvest or put food in barns because your heavenly Father feeds them. And you are far more valuable to him than they are (Matthew 6:25-26).

✓ Jesus taught that God's providence protects us from being separated from God:

My sheep recognize my voice; I know them, and they follow me. I give them eternal life, and they will never perish. No one will snatch them away from me, for my Father has given them to me, and he is more powerful than anyone else. So no one can take them from me (John 10:27-29).

✓ The Apostle Paul also explained that the providence of God preserves us from being separated from God.

And I am convinced that nothing can ever separate us from his love. Death can't, and life can't. The angels can't, and the demons can't. Our fears for today, our worries about tomorrow, and even the powers of hell can't keep God's love away.

> *Whether we are high above the sky or in the deepest ocean, nothing in all creation will ever be able to separate us from the love of God that is revealed in Christ Jesus our Lord* (Romans 8:38-39).

God's providence doesn't preserve us from dangers or problems. God never promises that we will avoid persecution and suffering. In fact, following God usually involves a degree of hardship, but these allow us to identify with Christ's sufferings:

> *Dear friends, don't be surprised at the fiery trials you are going through, as if something strange were happening to you. Instead, be very glad—because these trials will make you partners with Christ in his suffering, and afterward you will have the wonderful joy of sharing his glory when it is displayed to all the world* (1 Peter 4:12-13).

God's Providence Governs Our Activities

Another aspect of God's providence is His affirmative and proactive involvement in guiding and directing the course of events to fulfill His purposes. This aspect is sometimes referred to as God's *governing* activity.

His governing activity extends over:

- The elements of nature (Psalm 135:5-7)

- The animal creation (Psalm 104:21-29)

- Nations and governments (Daniel 2:21)

- The circumstances of individuals (1 Samuel 2:6-7)

Although God has the ability to intervene in all of the events of life, He does not dictate every occurrence that happens in your life. Much of what happens is just the logical progression of events or the laws of nature. God does not always intervene. Oftentimes He just allows events to happen. (To prove our point, pray that God will protect you from injury, and then drop a sledgehammer above your foot.) This means that we can't identify every single event in our life as being directed by God's providence. We still have to be responsible for the consequences of our own decisions (and our own stupidity). Within the realm of God's sovereignty, He still allows us the freedom to make our own choices (but you'll have to wait until Chapter 2 for more about that).

What's That Again?

1. Your desire to know and follow God's will is directly proportional to your belief that He knows what is best for you and is able to do something about it.

2. God is *omniscient* (all-knowing), *omnipotent* (all-powerful), and *omnipresent* (everywhere at the same time). These attributes make Him the perfect source for guidance.

3. By His sovereignty, God is in charge of what is happening in the universe and in your life.

4. The providence of God is His active participation in the events of your life. His providence includes our protection and preservation. It also extends to the governing of some of the circumstances in our lives.

Dig Deeper

It is impossible to adequately describe an infinite God, and we didn't have the chance to get very deep into the subject of God's nature. But if you are looking to God for guidance in your life, then you might want to dig deeper into His character. The more you know about Him, the better you'll feel about Him being in charge. Here are three books you might want to read:

- *Knowing God* by J. I. Packer. This book is considered a classic on the attributes of God.

- *Chosen by God* by R. C. Sproul. Dr. Sproul gives an excellent analytical explanation of God's sovereignty.

- *Does It Matter if God Exists?* by Millard J. Erickson. This book explains who God is and what He has done for us. That understanding is a good foundation for pursuing God's will for your life.

Moving On

If you have always prided yourself on being an independent and self-sufficient person, this may have been a tough chapter for you. You might be getting a bit fatalistic at this point. You might be thinking that it doesn't matter what you do in life or what choices you make because God is calling all of the shots. After all, His sovereignty puts

Him in control, and His governing activity has Him involved and active in all aspects of life. It's beginning to look like you are pretty dispensable.

But wait! God's sovereignty does not operate in a fashion that makes your freedom irrelevant. The exercise of your free will is not totally precluded by God's will. While divine sovereignty and human freedom may seem completely contradictory on the surface, that isn't how it works out. In the next chapter you'll see how much freedom God allows you to have. It may be more than you want.

CHAPTER 2

HEY GOD, WHAT DO YOU WANT FROM ME?

To walk out of His will is to walk into nowhere.

—C. S. Lewis

When it comes to knowing God's will for your life, the two most important ingredients are *God* and *you*. That's pretty obvious. What isn't so clear is that before you can think about yourself and what you want, you first have to think about God and what He wants. This generally applies to every situation you will ever encounter in your life.

It's only natural to want to know what God wants for you in the stuff that's crying out for your immediate attention, such as your education, your finances, your career, and your relationships. But before you can ask God to help you plan the structure of your life, you need to concentrate on building a solid foundation. If you're willing to learn how, God is more than willing to teach you.

Bruce & Stan

Chapter 2

Hey God, What Do You Want from Me?

Y ou're going to love this chapter, because we're going to tell you exactly what God's will is for your life. We're serious! No more sleepless nights wondering what God really wants from you. By the time you finish the next 23 pages, you're going to know. But before we discover what God's will is all about, we need to focus on *your* will.

Your will is an amazing thing. Without it, you would be little more than a machine that works according to someone else's design or input. With a will, you have the ability and the power to make decisions. Your determination and desire to do or not do certain things come from your will, and it starts the moment you are brought into this world. (Why do you think you cried three seconds after you were born? Some guy with rubber gloves and hairy arms took you *against your will* from the warm and safe confines of your mother's womb.)

Your Will and God's Will

Your will is so strong and so much a part of you that the way you view your will directly impacts the way you view God. Here's what we mean. Picture your will on a sliding scale with *Powerful* on one end and *Weak* on the other.

Strong Will—Weak God

Let's say you see yourself as a completely independent person. You do what you want when you want, and no one—not even God—is going to tell you how to run your life. Anything good in your life occurs because you make it happen. When bad stuff happens to you, it's up to you to fix things; God sure can't.

People who put their will above God's will see God as weak and somewhat powerless. Sure, He created the universe, but things seem like they're spinning out of His control, and there's nothing God can do about it. They live by the closing lines of William Ernest Henley's poem, *Invictus:*

> *It matters not how straight the gate,*
>   *How charged with punishment the scroll,*
> *I am the master of my fate;*
>   *I am the captain of my soul.*

Weak Will—Strong God

On the other end of the scale, let's say you think that your decisions don't matter much because other forces bigger than you are at work. The events and circumstances of your life have been predetermined, and there's not much you can do to change them. People who see things this way put God's will (which they sometimes refer to as "fate") way above their will because they see God as strong and capricious. After all, God made the universe, and He now runs everything with an iron fist. If bad things happen to you, it's because you ticked God off. If good things happen, then you've caught God on a good day. They live by the song made popular by Doris Day:

> *Que sera sera*
> *Whatever will be will be*
> *The future's not ours to see*
> *Que sera sera*

How Do You See God?

How do you see God? Be honest. Is He too weak to help you, or is He too strong to care about you? Are you comforted by the fact that God has the universe under control, or do you worry that God doesn't know what He's doing?

And how do you see yourself? Do you think you are completely free to make your own choices, good or bad—including the incredibly important decision to enter into a personal relationship with God—or do you think everything has been predetermined?

These difficult questions deserve your attention, because the way you view your own will impacts the way you see God and the way you live. It all gets very practical. That's why we want to help you develop a balanced picture of God in which you see Him as powerful enough to create and run the universe, but personal enough to care about you. It all starts with the way He created you.

God's Will and Free Will

One question about God's will that has been hotly debated is this:

> Are you really free to make your own choices, or are they predetermined by God and His will? In other words, do you have a free will?

The controversy over free will usually pits two opposing viewpoints against each other:

The Big Brother Viewpoint: Our Choices Are Determined

One of the most famous television commercials of all time introduced the Macintosh computer. The commercial ran only once—during the 1984 Super Bowl. This bleak vision of the future showed row upon row of people dressed alike in quasi-futuristic, bland clothing. They sat silently and stared at an enormous video screen as a giant head with coke-bottle glasses indoctrinated them. The commercial was meant to be an illustration of George Orwell's *1984,* a book that predicted a society in which people's choices would be limited to what "Big Brother" told them to do.

This view of free will is called *determinism.* This means we are forced to do things and make decisions based on external forces.

The Alice in Wonderland Viewpoint: It Doesn't Matter What We Choose

In Lewis Carroll's famous story, Alice asked the cat, "Would you tell me, please, which way I ought to go from here?" The cat replied, "That depends a good deal on where you want to get to." Alice then said, "I don't much care where," to which the cat then replied, "Then it doesn't matter which way you go."

Alice was illustrating the viewpoint of free will that says our choices don't really matter. And the reason they don't matter is that there's nothing or nobody influencing our choices. We are free to make decisions from a completely neutral and unbiased position and without any outside forces or personal inclinations.

 This view of free will is called *individualism*. It puts the responsibility completely on the individual to make choices. Since our choices aren't based on bias or prejudice, we are free to make decisions based on how we feel at the time.

The Reason Determinism Is Wrong

It's true that external forces can impact our world and sometimes limit our options, but they cannot destroy the human spirit. God has created us as beings bearing his image (Genesis 1:26-27), and He has given each one of us the desire to be involved in our own decisions. Outside forces may tell us how to behave or what to do, but they cannot make us enjoy something we don't want to do.

The Reason Individualism Is Wrong

This viewpoint of free will may sound good, but this is just as impossible as determinism. If you make choices from a completely neutral and unbiased position, it means you have no brain. You see, every single person has prejudices and biases, which could be lumped together in something called *desire*. Whenever you make choices, you do so because you *desire* to choose. Sometimes the desire is fairly intense, and other times you aren't even aware of it. But desire is always there.

Dr. R. C. Sproul explains that choice without desire is like an effect without a cause. It is something from nothing, and that's just impossible. Every effect has a cause, and every choice has a reason, and that reason comes from desire. "This is the very essence of free will" writes Dr. Sproul, "to choose according to our desires."

Another reason complete individualism is impossible is that God doesn't allow it. If you made decisions for no reason, then there would be no basis for right and wrong. Your choices would have no basis in morality, and there would be no way for God to evaluate them as good or bad. The Bible makes it clear that you are responsible for your decisions, and someday you are going to have to explain to God why you made the choices you did.

Nothing in all creation can hide from him. Everything is naked and exposed before his eyes. This is the God to whom we must explain all that we have done (Hebrews 4:13).

Back to the Garden

Does that verse from Hebrews remind you of anything? (The words *creation, hide,* and *naked* should give you a clue.) Give up? Think back to the Garden of Eden for a moment. Remember Adam and Eve, otherwise known as the First Parents? The true story of Adam and Eve as told in Genesis is your story as well. What they did provides a huge clue into this whole business of free will.

Created to Choose

If God had made Adam a robot and programmed him to obey everything He said, Adam would not have had a free will—and neither would you. But that's not the way God made the human race. He created people in His image with the natural ability to make choices. God explained this to Adam when he said, "You may freely eat any fruit in the garden except fruit from the tree of the knowledge of good and evil. If you eat of its fruit, you will surely die" (Genesis 2:16-17). Clearly God gave Adam a choice. God warned Adam about eating the fruit, but He did not restrict him. Adam's will was completely free.

Satan and Desire

Satan, the adversary of God and everything God created (*Satan* means "adversary"), challenged God's authority and wisdom. He told Adam and Eve that God didn't mean what He said. And then Satan tempted them at the point of their free will: *desire*. Remember, God told Adam that he would die if he ate the forbidden fruit. Satan told Adam just the opposite:

"You won't die!" the serpent hissed. "God knows that your eyes will be opened when you eat it. You will become just like God, knowing everything, both good and evil" (Genesis 3:4-5).

Satan's strategy worked (by the way, he hasn't changed his strategy since), and Adam and Eve gave in to temptation at the point of their desire. They willfully chose to disobey God, and the reason was that they wanted to be just like God. Sin entered the world for the first time and infected the human race. Suddenly aware of their corruption, Adam and Eve tried to cover up and hide from God. It didn't work then, and it doesn't work now (read Hebrews 4:13 again).

LEARN THE LINGO The word *sin* in Hebrew (the original language of the Old Testament) means "falling away from *or* missing the right path." When you sin, you literally fall away from God and miss the right path He has marked for you.

A Fine Mess

It's too easy to blame Adam and Eve for getting you into this sin mess. Yes, they blew it, but we are no different than they were. Just like our First Parents, we are free to make choices because that's the way God created us. We can freely choose to obey God and follow His will, or we can disobey God and what He wants us to do. We don't have to give in to sin, and when we do, it's because we choose to sin.

DID GOD SET THE HUMAN RACE UP FOR THE FALL?

Some people argue that God set the human race up for the Fall. In other words, Adam and Eve had no choice but to sin. But that just doesn't make sense. God could have created us humans as robots who had no choice but to obey Him, or He could have created us as people who could freely obey or disobey Him (which He did). There's no third option that says God created us to sin by disobeying Him. Adam and Eve had a free will, and so does every person born since then. They freely chose to disobey God.

Whatever Became of Sin?

In case you haven't noticed, people don't seem to take sin seriously these days. You would think that people would be very conscious of God and their sinful rebellion against Him. But most people treat sin as if it's out of their hands. It's rare to hear someone say, "I sinned," or even, "I was wrong." You are more likely to hear, "Mistakes were made," or "I couldn't help it." Even people who claim to be Christians, who are just as vulnerable to sin as everyone else, have a hard time admitting their sin. Why is this?

The answer goes back to free will. After the Fall, humanity still has the ability to choose God or not choose God. Our free will is intact, but with one difference (and it's a BIG difference). We have the *freedom* to choose God, but we no longer have the *desire* (Romans 3:11).

Desiring and Choosing God

We have come to a critical part of God's will. You need to understand this before you can know and do God's will:

> Before you can know God's will,
> you have to have a desire for
> God's will. And before you have
> a desire for God's will, you have
> to have a desire for God.

You may think that everyone wants to
know God's will, but that isn't true. Only
those people who freely desire God have
a desire to know God and His will. But
how do you get the desire for God? It's
really quite simple. God gives you the
desire, and it involves Jesus and the Holy
Spirit.

Here's an illustration of how this works.
Imagine that Jesus is standing in the
middle of a field, and all the people of the
world (including you) are running away
from Him (this is accurate because all the
people in the world are naturally sinful,
and sinful people naturally run from God).
The only way that we will turn around and
run toward God is when God uses the Holy
Spirit to convince us that we are sinful
(John 16:8-9). It's as if God grabs us by the
shoulders, brings us to a screeching halt,
and turns us around to look squarely in the
face of Jesus.

Our act of turning away from sin and toward Christ is called *repentance.* But it's not enough to repent. You also have to *respond* by an act of your free will. The Holy Spirit must turn us toward Christ, but we have to make the decision to believe and accept Him (John 3:16).

If this is difficult to understand, don't worry. You're in good company. Even Jesus' own disciples had trouble with the idea of turning back to Jesus. They said, "This is very hard to understand. How can anyone accept it?" (John 6:60).

Ever the patient teacher, Jesus explained, "It is the Spirit who gives eternal life. Human effort accomplishes nothing" (John 6:63). Then he told them the conditions for coming to Him.

> *This is what I meant when I said that people can't come to me unless the Father brings them to me* (John 6:65).

Desiring God's Will

Something wonderful happens when we make the choice to follow God by believing in Jesus: God changes each of us into a new person. Before we accept God's free gift of salvation, we have no desire for God, and we have no desire to know and do God's will. However, once we respond to God, He changes our desires. For the first time in our lives, we want to know what God wants us to do.

God saved you by his special favor when you believed. And you can't take credit for this; it is a gift from God. Salvation is not a reward for the good things we have done, so none of us can boast about it. For we are God's masterpiece. He has created us anew in Christ Jesus, so that we can do the good things he planned for us long ago (Ephesians 2:8-10).

What God Wants You to Do

Okay, here it is. The part you've been waiting for. We're going to tell you exactly what God wants you to do. We know with absolute certainty God's will for your life. The reason we can say this is that God has said so Himself in the Bible, His personal message to all people everywhere.

Think of these as "basic principles for knowing God's will." Another way to look at it is that these are *prerequisites* to knowing God's will more specifically. Just like you can't skip over the required courses if you want to get a college degree, you can't skip over these basic principles if you want to know more of what God wants you to do.

1. God wants you to believe in Jesus and accept Him as your Savior.

This is Number One on God's list of things He wants you to do. Contrary to what many people believe about God, He doesn't want anyone to die in their sins and apart from knowing Him personally through Jesus. The love of God compelled Him to send His only Son to die for our sins. All we have to do is believe.

> *For God so loved the world that he gave his only Son, so that everyone who believes in him will not perish but have eternal life* (John 3:16).

> *He does not want anyone to perish, so he is giving more time for everyone to repent* (2 Peter 3:9).

2. *God wants you to have eternal life.*

God created humanity to be in relationship with Him—forever. Sin broke that relationship, but you can get back with God by believing in Jesus. Not only will you not die spiritually, but you will also live forever. This is God's will for everyone who believes in Jesus, who said:

> *For it is my Father's will that all who see his Son and believe in him should have eternal life—that I should raise them at the last day* (John 6:40).

3. *God wants you to be like Jesus.*

God doesn't want you to accept Jesus and then live your life like you always have. His will for you is to be like Jesus, to live your life the way Jesus did and to do the things that Jesus said.

> *Those who say they live in God should live their lives as Christ did* (1 John 2:6).

4. *God wants you to love Him.*

A lawyer once asked Jesus to give him the most important commandment. Here's what Jesus said:

> *You must love the Lord your God with all your heart, all your soul, and all your mind. This is the first and greatest commandment* (Matthew 22:37-38).

5. God wants you to love others.

The most important commandment is tied to the second most important commandment. You can't have one without the other.

> *Love your neighbor as yourself* (Matthew 22:39).

6. God wants you to obey Him.

Loving someone and doing what pleases them go hand in hand. Your love for God should compel you to want to do what He wants you to do.

> *Obey God because you are his children. Don't slip back into your old ways of doing evil; you didn't know any better then* (1 Peter 1:14).

7. God wants you to change the way you think.

It's so easy—even as a Christian—to get caught up in the way everybody else does things. God wants something much different from you, and it starts with changing your mental orientation.

> *Don't copy the behavior and customs of this world, but let God transform you into a new person by changing the way you think. Then you will know what God wants you to do, and you will know how good and pleasing and perfect his will really is* (Romans 12:2).

8. God wants you to know Him better.

Knowing God is a lifelong challenge that will enrich your life every single day. But God won't force Himself on you. It's up to you to learn more about God and what He wants you to do. Here's what the Apostle Paul wrote to some first-century Christians:

> *We ask God to give you a complete under-standing of what he wants to do in your lives, and we ask him to make you wise with spiritual wisdom. Then the way you live will always honor and please the Lord, and you will continually do good, kind things for others. All the while, you will learn to know God better and better* (Colossians 1:9-10).

9. God wants you to submit to Him.

As you become more like Christ each day, you will lead a moral, loving life that is in submission to God. This is a big part of God's will for your life.

> *The Lord has already told you what is good, and this is what he requires: to do what is right, to love mercy, and to walk humbly with your God* (Micah 6:8).

10. God wants you to do His will.

This may sound redundant, but think of this last principle as a summary of all the others. God wants you to think about doing His will all the time. The message that Moses gave to the nation of Israel applies to us today:

> *And now, Israel, what does the Lord your God require of you? He requires you to fear him, to live according to his will, to love and worship him with all your heart and soul, and to obey the Lord's commands and laws that I am giving you today for your own good* (Deuteronomy 10:12-13).

What's That Again?

1. The way you view your will directly impacts the way you view God's will.

2. God created you in His image, and He has given you the desire to make your own decisions. The Bible makes it clear that God holds you responsible for the choices you make.

3. God has given you a free will, but sin has corrupted your desire to freely choose God and His will. Only God can change your desire for Him by turning you around so you can see Jesus.

4. The greatest thing God wants is for you to accept Jesus as your personal Savior. He wants to give you eternal life, and He wants you to be like Jesus.

5. God wants you to love Him, and He wants you to love others. God wants you to obey Him, and He wants you to change the way you think.

6. God wants you to know Him better, and He wants you to submit to Him.

7. In summary, God wants you to do His will.

Dig Deeper

One of the reasons we write our *Pocket Guides* is to get you interested in a subject so you will learn more about it by doing more study. Here are some books to start with:

- *Invisible Hand* by R. C. Sproul. Do things "just happen" in your life, or do they happen for a reason? This book gives the answer.

- *The Will of God as a Way of Life* by Gerald L. Sittser. This is an extremely practical book that shows how God actively guides you in the present circumstances of your life.

- *Affirming the Will of God* by Paul E. Little. A classic little booklet (even shorter than this one) that makes a lot of sense.

Moving On

If you are anxious to get some guidance about some specific things in your life, such as your career, your finances, and your relationships, then all you have to do is turn the page. In the next chapter we're going to tell you how following the basic principles for knowing God's will can help you with the everyday choices in your life.

CHAPTER 3

IT'S NOT A GAME OF HIDE-AND-SEEK

*Where God has put a period,
do not change it to a question mark.*

—T. J. Bach

We admit that we teased you a bit in the last chapter. We told you that we were going to tell you exactly what God's will is for your life. And in a way, we did that. Only we weren't much help in the specific areas of your life. That's what this chapter is all about.

We know you want to discover God's specific will for your life, and we are about to tell you what it is. Really!

If you are like most people, you have been frustrated because God hasn't been giving you clear signals about choices in your life. Well, get ready to say goodbye to your frustration because God's isn't trying to hide His will from you. In fact, He has made it pretty easy to find. You just have to know what you are looking for.

Bruce & Stan

Chapter 3

It's Not a Game of Hide-and-Seek

You have spent your entire life playing guessing games. It started when you were an infant and your parents pestered you with that annoying "peek-a-boo" game. As a toddler, you were humiliated with the "guess which hand is holding the candy" game. By the time you were in elementary school, you suffered the indignity of searching for your older siblings in a game of "hide-and-seek," only to learn that they ditched you while you were counting to 100. Now you are much older, and the guessing still continues, whether it involves picking stocks on the NASDAQ or trying to find a missing sock that's not in the dryer.

Admit it. You have always been frustrated by these guessing games, but they seem to be a part of life. But when it comes to finding God's will, you thought you'd get a break because He would reveal it to you. But He hasn't, and you're stuck guessing at it.

God Isn't Hiding, and Neither Is His Will

We've got good news for you. God doesn't like to play games. (We don't mean that He is opposed to sports. In fact, we've told our wives that God is a sports fanatic, which is why we have to watch so many games on TV.) When we say that He doesn't play games, we mean that He isn't trying to psych you out. God isn't trying to mess with your mind.

God doesn't try to hide from people. He has promised that He will reveal Himself to you if you are looking for Him.

> *"If you look for me in earnest, you will find me when you seek me. I will be found by you," says the Lord* (Jeremiah 29:13-14).

God even makes His existence obvious to people who aren't necessarily looking for Him.

> *From the time the world was created, people have seen the earth and sky and all that God made. They can clearly see his invisible qualities—his eternal power and divine nature. So they have no excuse whatsoever for not knowing God* (Romans 1:20).

Just as God makes Himself conspicuous (it is hard to hide when you are omnipresent), He takes the same approach with revealing His will. He isn't hiding it. He actually is anxious for you to find it.

> *He leads the humble in what is right, teaching them his way* (Psalm 25:9).

> *The Lord says, "I will guide you along the best pathway for your life. I will advise you and watch over you"* (Psalm 32:8).

You've Got to Know What You Are Looking For

Let's get one thing straight: God has a will for your life. That fact is made obvious from verses like these:

> *We ask God to give you a complete understanding of what he wants to do in your lives* (Colossians 1:9).

> *Teach me to do your will, for you are my God* (Psalm 143:10).

> *Don't act thoughtlessly, but try to understand what the Lord wants you to do* (Ephesians 5:17).

So, if God has a will for your life, and if He wants you to know it, then why are you having so much trouble finding it? Well, it just may be that you are looking for the wrong thing. Maybe you and God have different ideas of what His will looks like. Maybe God's will is sitting right in front of you, but you aren't recognizing it.

Let's analyze God's will to see what we are talking about. It seems to break down into three different components: a sovereign plan for the universe, a moral code for all of humanity, and a general plan for your life.

God's Sovereign Plan

God has a plan for the universe. Before He created the world, He planned exactly how things were going to turn out. It was more than just knowing in advance how random events were going to turn out. As we discussed in Chapter 1, God is in control, and all events operate within the context of His exact plan. The result will be what He has intended all along.

For the most part, God's sovereign plan is hidden and unknown to us. Oh, sure, we know a little bit about it because we can learn from what has happened in the past, and the Bible tells us a little bit about what is going to happen in the future. (What a convenient opportunity to put in a shameless plug for *Bruce & Stan's® Guide to Bible Prophecy*.) God doesn't expect us to understand—or even "find"—His sovereign plan. It is just enough that we know that He has one and that He is in control.

Oh, what a wonderful God we have! How great are his riches and wisdom and knowledge! How impossible it is for us to understand his decisions and his methods! For who can know what the Lord is thinking?...For everything comes from him; everything exists by his power and is intended for his glory (Romans 11:33-36).

God's Moral Code

Another aspect of God's will includes the moral code that He has established for all of humanity. This moral code is simply God's standard of behavior and conduct that is set forth in the Bible. We aren't talking about a set of dos and don'ts that must be strictly followed. God's moral code is mostly about principles that are beneficial for you. Things like "love your neighbor" and "always be thankful."

God expects us to know the principles of His moral code. You won't have any trouble finding them. They are in the Bible. It is just a matter of reading them and then *obeying* them. We shouldn't consider it a hardship to follow these general principles because we will be much better off if we do.

Obey all the laws Moses gave you. Do not turn away from them, and you will be successful in everything you do. Study this Book of the Law continually. Meditate on it day and night so you may be sure to obey all that is written in it. Only then will you succeed (Joshua 1:7-8).

God's General Will for Your Life

Here we go. Now things are becoming very interesting because it is getting to be all about *you*. We know you are giddy with anticipation for us to reveal to you God's will for your life. And we are going to do it—we promise. But first, we need to refresh your memory a bit. (We know that in the excitement of discovering God's will at long last, you might have forgotten a few things from Chapter 2).

- God wants you to believe in Jesus and accept Him as your Savior (John 3:16; 2 Peter 3:9).

- God wants you to be like Jesus (1 John 2:6).

- God wants you to know Him better and to submit to Him (Colossians 1:9-10; Micah 6:8).

Within those parameters of what God wants, we can boldly and confidently pronounce God's will for your life. Are you ready? Drum roll, please.

> It is God's will for your life that you have a growing relationship with Him that makes you more like Christ each day.

Are you feeling cheated? You were probably expecting some *specifics*. We will get to the specifics of your life in just a moment. But for now, we are talking about God's *general* will for your life. It is not difficult to figure out God's will for you. It is simply knowing what He wants from you. As we set forth at the end of Chapter 2 and briefly summarized above, God wants a relationship with you and He wants you to be engaged in the process of becoming more Christlike. It is as simple as that. That is God's will for you.

God's will is not about a place, or a thing, or a time. God's will is all about the condition of your heart. That's what God really cares about. We overlook that fact when we trivialize God's will by thinking that it primarily applies to choosing between Coke or Pepsi, boxers or briefs, and decisions relating to career.

- God's will is more about your *character* than it is about making choices.

- God's will is more about your *attitude* than it is about finding answers.

- God's will is more about your *relationship* with God than it is about getting results.

And Now to the Specifics

We promised you that we would get to the specifics, and now we will. After all, we know that you have specific questions, and you need to make some specific decisions. There may be issues in your life that involve your family, your friendship, your education, your career, or your finances. They may be somewhat mundane (Should I buy or lease my next car?), or they may be monumental (Is this the person I should marry?). We don't know your personal situation, but we know that you are looking to God for some specific direction.

Since you are interested in specific direction from God, you were probably disappointed when we explained that God's will for you is about your relationship with Him rather than results. Don't despair. As your relationship with God grows deeper, you will begin to think like He does. That new way of thinking will help you make decisions about the specific issues you are facing.

And so, dear Christian friends, I plead with you to give your bodies to God. Let them be a living and holy sacrifice— the kind he will accept. When you think of what he has done for you, is this too much to ask? Don't copy the behavior and customs of this world, but let God transform you into a new person by changing the way you think. Then you will know what God wants you to do, and you will know how good and pleasing and perfect his will really is (Romans 12:1-2).

What God's Will Is All About

Notice again the three components of God's will:

1. God's sovereign plan for the universe
2. God's moral code for humanity
3. God's general will for you

Notice that God doesn't have a specific, explicit, and detailed will for your life that involves your choices on everything from breakfast cereals to colleges. In some respects, that may make your life a little more difficult because many decisions are left up to you. On the other hand, you have freedom to make decisions within a wide range options (limited only by the parameters of God's moral code).

What God's Will Is Not

We know you might be a bit disappointed to learn that God does not have a specific will for every issue in your life. Perhaps you were frustrated because you couldn't make decisions in your life, and you wanted God to provide the answers. Maybe your anxiety wasn't caused by your inability to choose; maybe you were just afraid that there was only one correct choice within God's will, and you didn't want to blow it.

Unfortunately, many people mistakenly believe that God's will is always very specific and limited to a single choice. That erroneous viewpoint misrepresents God's will. If you think that there is only one correct choice to any decision, then you will mistakenly view God's will like:

✓ *A Tightrope.* You have to walk carefully along God's will. You can't move too quickly, and all of your mental energy is focused on using that long pole to maintain your balance. Your situation is so precarious that you can't enjoy the walk. If you make the slightest misstep, you will have a tragic fall (which could prove to be fatal if you impale yourself on your balancing pole).

✓ *A Maze.* Your life is a series of dead-ends and wrong turns. You can't go very far in life without being confronted with a choice of turning left or right. You know that you have a 50–50 chance of being wrong. A few wrong turns in a row and you'll be regressing instead of making progress. Sooner or later, you are bound to be trapped or lost. Life is pretty discouraging because you know you'll never be successful at routing directly through God's will.

✓ *A Bean Under the Cup.* This is when God's will is that game in which a huckster places a bean under one of three cups; you see the bean as it is covered up, but then the cups are moved around with hands that move quicker than a Cuisinart. When the hands stop spinning, you've got to guess which cup is hiding God's will. You're fairly sure that you know where God's will is, but your guess is invariably wrong. You feel like a big loser (and you are sure that you hear God snickering).

Fortunately for us, God doesn't take sadistic pleasure in watching us sweat through the process of finding His will.

God's Will Is About Guidance, Not Guessing

God's will is not some narrow tightrope, and we don't have to guess about it. Rather, it is all about the freedom to make choices within certain broad parameters. Those boundaries are His moral code. As long as our decisions do not violate Scriptural principles, we are free to make whatever choice seems best to us. There may be many acceptable answers, and we don't need to worry that our decision will derail us from God's only preferred route.

When you think about it, the freedom God gives to us to make any choice within the bounds of His moral code is consistent with God's role. The Bible describes God as our King, our Father, and our Shepherd. Using those analogies, it is natural to expect that we would be given some decision-making freedom.

- ✓ *As a King.* An evil dictator oppresses the citizens and gives them little freedom. They are told where to go and what to do. In contrast, a good king gives his subjects much freedom. While there may be rules in the king-dom for the beneficial functioning of the community, each subject can enjoy life without oppression.

- ✓ *As a Father.* It is the goal of every father to raise his children to maturity. He doesn't want them to stay at an imma-ture stage in which their every move must be watched. Part of the teaching process includes giving the child the freedom to make mistakes. With increasing maturity comes additional freedom. Eventually, the children will become wise enough to make deci-sions on their own. (In real life, matu-rity does not always coincide with getting a driver's license, but we aren't sure how that fits into the "God's will" analogy.)

✓ *As a Shepherd.* The shepherd is responsible for making sure that the sheep have food to eat. How does that happen? The shepherd leads them to a field. Within the boundaries of that field, the sheep move around. They eat where they want. The shepherd doesn't point out each edible blade of grass. The sheep might consume a few briars or bristles, but that is okay because they will learn what to avoid in the future (or suffer the gastro-intestinal consequences). When it comes to moving to the next field, the sheep don't have to walk in single file fashion behind the shepherd. They meander along, but the shepherd's sheep dog makes sure they don't go too far astray.

We don't want to push these analogies too far. But you can see that God's moral code is similar to a king's laws, a curfew imposed by a father, or a pasture fence (maybe the comparison to the sheep dog is stretching it). As long as we are operating within those parameters, we enjoy the freedom to make choices, and any such choice is acceptable to God.

God's Will Is a Circle, Not a Dot

In his book, *Decision Making and the Will of God*, Garry Friesen uses the images of a circle and a dot to illustrate God's will. He uses a circle to represent God's moral code. Operating outside of the circle means that you are outside of God's will. But all decisions that fall within the circumference of the circle are acceptable to God (because they are within His moral code).

The premise of Friesen's book is that many people mistakenly believe that God has a limited, specific will for most of life's decisions. He uses a dot to illustrate this viewpoint. As he diagrams it, Friesen puts a dot in the center of the circle to represent the approach, which assumes that God has a specific will for every issue.

Friesen rejects the notion that we should be looking for a "dot" of God's will in each decision. Here is how he explains it:

> Scripture indicates that an area of freedom where genuine opportunity

of choice is granted to the believer should replace the dot. For God's children, all things within the moral will of God are lawful, clean and pure. In decisions that are made within that moral will, the Christian should not feel guilty about his choice; neither should he fear that his decision is unacceptable to God. God has made it clear what He wants: His plan for His children is for them to enjoy the freedom that He has granted. It is a freedom that is clearly established in Scripture from the nature of laws, the nature of sin, and direct statements of the Bible.

Here is the bottom line: Stop searching for God's will like it is a tiny dot. Dots are difficult to find, and God isn't trying to make His will like a buried treasure. Think of God's will as a circle in which you are free to make decisions. The more you develop your relationship with God, the easier it will be for you to make those decisions because you'll be approaching them from God's perspective.

WHAT ABOUT THE EXAMPLES IN THE BIBLE WHEN GOD EXPRESSED HIS SPECIFIC WILL?

It would be wrong to say that God has never expressed a specific will. The Bible reports several instances in which God had a specific will for the life of a certain individual, and God made it plainly known to that person. Here are a few examples:

- God spoke His specific will to Balaam through a talking donkey (Numbers 22).

- God gave specific instruction to Moses at the burning bush (Exodus 3).

- An angel brought the message of God's will to Joseph regarding his marriage to Mary (Matthew 1).

- God told Peter in a dream that Peter should travel to the house of Cornelius (Acts 10).

These examples appear to be the exception rather than the rule. Each time God's specific will is reported in the Bible, the circumstances are highly unusual. Don't expect that God is going to communicate His specific will to you through a talking donkey. (But if He does, pay close attention.)

What's That Again?

1. God wants you to know what His will is.

2. God has a sovereign plan for the universe, a moral code for humanity, and a general will for your life.

3. God's general will for your life is that you have a growing relationship with Him, which makes you more like Christ each day.

4. God's will is more about *who* you are than it is about where you go or what you do. God's will is all about your relationship with Him.

5. God's will is not a tightrope, a maze, or a bean under a cup. God's will allows you the freedom to make any choice that falls within His moral code.

6. God's will is a circle; it is not a dot.

Dig Deeper

- The whole circle/dot analogy can be found in *Decision Making and the Will of God* by Garry Friesen. This book does a great job of exposing some of the misconceptions about God's will.

- *The Fight* by John White is a book that discusses the practical aspects of Christian living. The chapter entitled "Guidance" has an excellent discussion of God's will.

- There are several chapters in *The Man in the Mirror* by Patrick M. Morley that address the subject of God's will. Although the book is subtitled *Solving the 24 Problems Men Face*, it isn't as gender-specific as the subtitle suggests. The issues pertaining to God's will are the same whether you have two X chromosomes or the XY combination.

Moving On

This might have been a "good news/bad news" chapter. It is good news that God's will allows you to make any decision within God's moral code. However, it might be bad news that you are still stuck with having to make a decision. Don't despair. God has given you some very practical assistance to help with that task.

Chapter 4

God Is Pointing the Way

In His will is our peace.

—Dante Alighieri

BRUCE & STAN SAY

Have you ever been out to eat with someone who can't decide what to order? With no difficulty and little fanfare, everyone else at the table tells the server what they want, but this one guy hems and haws and asks all kinds of questions about the menu (which the server patiently answers), and still he can't decide. He even looks at the next table, points to a plate of food and asks, "What's that? Is that any good?" It goes on like this until the other people (including the server) are ready to strangle him. You want to yell out, "Pick something! Just make a decision!"

It's one thing to struggle with your food selection at the Cracker Barrel, and quite another to be indecisive about the things that really matter in life. Yet that's what a lot of people do. Rather than developing the skills to make intelligent, effective decisions, they solve their problems and confront their opportunities by putting their decisions off, or worse, not making them at all.

As you finish this book, we want to give you some practical guidelines for knowing God's will that will help you make good decisions throughout your life.

Bruce & Stan

Chapter 4

God Is Pointing the Way

What's Ahead

➤ Three Things Everyone Can Do Every Day
➤ Seven Resources of God's Will
➤ Two Traps to Avoid

*A*classic example of good decision making took place years ago in a television commercial. The scene opens with two boys sitting around the breakfast table, each with a bowl of Life cereal in front of them. The boys are skeptical. They want to eat, but they've never tried Life cereal. What if it doesn't taste good? Then one boy gets a bright idea. He gets Mikey, his little brother, and asks him to try the cereal, because "Mikey hates everything." So they shove a bowl of Life in front of Mikey and watch as the little guy dips his spoon into the bowl.

You know how the commercial ends. Mikey keeps eating his bowl of Life, causing the older boys to look at each other and exclaim, "He likes it!" The problem of the mystery cereal is solved, the boys dig in with relish (and some milk), and a classic commercial is born. As for the lesson in decision making, the Mikey commercial follows the classic procedure known as "From Problem to Decision," which goes like this:

- *Identify the problem*
  The problem is that the two boys are hungry, but they don't want to risk eating a bad-tasting cereal.

- *Gather information*
  The boys enlist Mikey to try the cereal.

- *Evaluate the evidence*
  Clearly Mikey likes the cereal.

- *Consider your choices*

The boys could watch Mikey finish off
this obviously good-tasting cereal, or
they could start eating it themselves.

- *Choose and implement the best alternative*
  The boys decide to eat the cereal, and
  Life becomes a favorite of children
  everywhere.

Finding God's Everyday Will

If only decisions in life were so simple. If
only the practical, everyday process of
knowing what God wants you to do were
as straightforward as "From Problem to
Decision."

As a matter of fact, the practical, everyday
process of finding what God wants you to
do is simple and straightforward. We're
not going to tell you it's *easy*, because
making good decisions can be a challenge.
But there are some reliable and proven
methods you can use to solve the problems
and take advantage of the opportunities
that enter your life on a regular basis. And
they all relate to finding and doing God's
everyday will.

What Is God's Everyday Will?

The way we see it, there are two aspects of God's will. There is God's *eternal* will, which concerns stuff like: accepting Jesus as your Savior, becoming more like Jesus and living with Jesus forever in heaven, and telling other people about Jesus and what He's done for you (John 3:16; Ephesians 1:4-5; Mark 16:15). God wants these eternal benefits for all people. Then there is God's *everyday* will, which involves all the relationships, the circumstances, and the locations of your life. These are different for all people. Although God knows all about you, including the decisions you make every day, He has left it to you to make the choices—big and small—that impact your life. God wants to be involved in the details of your life (Psalm 37:23), but He has given you the mind and the will to make your own decisions. You are never out of God's sovereign care, but He has given you the freedom to discover what He wants for you every day of your life. This is what we mean by God's everyday will.

Three Things Everyone Can Do Every Day

Each day of your life is filled with choices and decisions. Some decisions you make automatically (like brushing your teeth), while others take more time and thought (like starting a new business). You may not see the results of your more thoughtful decisions for days, months, or even years, but at some point the consequences of what you decide at any given moment are played out. People are affected, events are impacted, and circumstances are set into motion.

God isn't concerned with the kind of toothpaste you use, but He does care about your new business. He cares about each decision you make to establish your business and build it into a success. God wants your everyday decisions to line up with His everyday will. You get to decide, but God wants you to focus on Him each step of the way. Here are three things you can do to keep all your decisions in the context of God's will:

1. Commit to do the will of God.

Do you want to find God's will in a particular situation? Then don't play "Let's Make a Deal" with God. Don't say to God, "Tell me what your will is, and then I'll decide if I want to do it or not." God doesn't play that game, so don't play that game with God. In his little book, *How to Know the Will of God,* Russ Johnston wrote: "God does not reveal His will to curiosity seekers." If you're curious rather than serious about God's everyday will, you'll never know what it is.

Committing to the will of God involves trusting God. You have to trust that God has your best interests in mind at all times. He knows you better than you know yourself, and He knows what's best for you. God knows your weaknesses, and He knows your strengths. God knows your fears, and He knows your hopes. God will never mislead you or do you harm. We've already given you this verse, but it's so good we don't mind repeating it:

> *"For I know the plans I have for you,"*
> *says the Lord. "They are plans for good*

*and not for disaster, to give you a future
and a hope"* (Jeremiah 29:11).

Trusting God for your future—whether
that future is tomorrow or ten years from
now—begins with trusting God now. And
you don't have to wait long for the payoff.
Once you have committed to do God's
will—regardless of what it is—God will
show you what it is step-by-step.

> *Trust in the Lord with all your heart; do
> not depend on your own understanding.
> Seek his will in all you do, and he will
> direct your paths* (Proverbs 3:5-6).

2. See things from God's perspective.

You know how important it is to get a
"bird's eye" view of things. Before you
explore New York at ground level, it's
important to study a map so you can find
your way around. Before you decide to
major in quantum physics, you need to
read the course descriptions so you can
determine if your strengths fit the require-
ments. The same principle applies to God's
everyday will: You need to get a "God's
eye" view before you can do it.

This is going to sound a little contradictory, but hear us out. When you insist on doing God's will from *your* perspective, then your main concern is *doing.* You get caught up in your own performance. By contrast, when you do God's will from *His* perspective, you are more concerned about *being.* God wants you to do stuff for Him, but He's more interested in the kind of person you are becoming than the specific things you are doing. He knows that when your *being* is right, then your *doing* will be right. And when your *doing* is right, then God gets the credit He deserves, no matter what it is you're doing.

> *Whatever you eat or drink or whatever you do, you must do all for the glory of God* (1 Corinthians 10:31).

3. Let God work in you.

The final thing God wants you to know before you do His everyday will is that you don't have to do it all by yourself. God has promised to help you.

> *For God is working in you, giving you the desire to obey him and the power to do what pleases him* (Philippians 2:13).

What would you do if Bill Gates came to you and said, "I believe in you so much that I'm going to put all of my wealth and power at your disposal to help you succeed"? Would you accept Bill's offer (even if you don't do Windows)? Of course you would!

So here's God (whose wealth and power make Mr. Gates' resources look like a pimple on an elephant's backside), and he's saying, "I believe in you so much that I'm going to put all of my resources at your disposal to help you succeed." Should you accept God's offer? Absolutely!

> *I pray that from his glorious, unlimited resources he will give you mighty inner strength through his Holy Spirit. And I pray that Christ will be more and more at home in your hearts as you trust him* (Ephesians 3:16-17).

Seven Resources of God's Will

Make no mistake about it. Making wise decisions in the context of God's will isn't easy. Often it's complicated. Sometimes it's frustrating. But just like anything worth doing, God's will is always rewarding. Even if you aren't certain about what your next move should be, you can trust God that He will never lead you astray. God may not reveal his everyday will when you think you need it, but He will show you when He knows you need it. Be patient. Wait for God's best.

Having said that, you don't have to sit around wondering what to do next. Waiting for God's best doesn't mean that you do nothing. You have the freedom to use your thoughtful judgment, your previous experience, and your current research to make wise decisions in the context of God's will.

You also have the freedom to bring God into the decision-making process at each step. Does this mean you should look into the sky, ask God for advice, and then listen for Him to respond each time you need to make a decision? Well, there are worse things you could do, but we were thinking along more practical lines. Remember, God's will is more about guidance than guessing. God isn't a fortune-teller, and neither is He a divine dictator. God is your guide, and He has given you the resources you need to make wise decisions in the context of His will for your life.

YOU'RE TIGER WOODS

You may not use all of these God-centered resources each time you are faced with a decision, but you need to get really good at using all of them. Think of your life as a golf course, and you're Tiger Woods. You aren't going to use each club in your bag for every hole, but you need to be ready to use each club when you need it, and that takes daily practice. In the same way you need to "practice" God's will by drawing on these resources every day.

The Word of God

Most of God's everyday will for you is contained in His Word, the Bible, and that's because the Bible is God's personal message for you. This is the way God talks to you. People who don't know God's Word don't know God's will. They don't know the essential things God wants for them because they don't read the Bible regularly and they don't study it systematically.

Don't make this mistake. The Word of God is your primary source of guidance.

> *Your word is a lamp for my feet and a light for my path* (Psalm 119:105).

The Bible contains many direct principles, which Chuck Swindoll calls "specific, black-and-white truths that take all the guesswork out of the way." Here's an example:

> *Let there be no sexual immorality, impurity, or greed among you. Such sins have no place among God's people. Obscene stories, foolish talk, and coarse jokes—these are not for you* (Ephesians 5:3).

There's no gray area there, and the Bible is full of such specifics. If you are doing anything that contradicts these principles, then you can be sure you are out of the will of God. And even if the Bible doesn't give you a black-and-white answer about something you are going to encounter, you'll find plenty of general guidelines to help you navigate through the gray areas of your life. Here's an example:

For though your hearts were once full of darkness, now you are full of light from the Lord, and your behavior should show it. For this light within you produces only what is good and right and true (Ephesians 5:8-9).

Finding and following God's will requires spiritual maturity and good judgment, which come when you know God's Word.

Talking with God

If God talks to you through the Bible, then the way you talk with God is through prayer. King David wrote, "The Lord will answer when I call to him" (Psalm 4:3). "Devote yourselves to prayer," wrote the Apostle Paul (Colossians 4:2). And Jesus, who spent more time in prayer than anyone else, said, "Keep asking, and you will be given what you ask for" (Matthew 7:7).

Do you wonder what you should do in a particular

> *Has it ever struck you that the vast majority of the will of God for your life has already been revealed in the Bible? That is a crucial thing to grasp.*
>
> —*Paul Little*

situation? Pray to God about it. Ask Him for an answer. But realize this: If you want to know God's will for you, you need to pray according to His will.

> *And we can be confident that he will listen to us whenever we ask him for anything in line with his will* (1 John 5:14).

This isn't a circular argument. This doesn't mean that you need to know God's will for a particular situation before you ask God to reveal His will to you. Praying according to God's will means praying according to Scripture. It means you will never ask God for something you know is contradictory to His nature or His Word. Praying according to God's will also means praying with faith, trusting that God has your best interest in mind at all times.

> *The earnest prayer of a righteous person has great power and wonderful results* (James 5:16).

The Spirit of God

When it comes to knowing and doing God's will, the Holy Spirit is your secret weapon. He's the inside source "who leads into all truth" (John 14:17). Sometimes the word "prompting" is used to describe the Holy Spirit's work in your life. Here's what it means. Think of "prompting" in the sense of "control," because when you let the Holy Spirit control you (Ephesians 5:18), then you are giving your whole life over to God, so that whatever you do, you are doing it in the will of God and to the glory of God (1 Corinthians 10:31). If you are walking in the light by reading your Bible, and you are talking with God through prayer, then you are also in the Holy Spirit's control, and your inner promptings are more likely to be God speaking to you.

The Work of God

At any given moment you are connected to a variety of people, places, and events; and they are constantly changing. Your life is fluid, not stationary. If you want to know God's will for you today, you need to be aware of what's going on around you. "Look around you!" Jesus told his disciples. "Vast fields are ripening all around us and are ready now for the harvest" (John 4:35). As someone who is eager to do God's will, you need to open your eyes today and see where God is working.

This gets us back to the picture of God's will as a circle rather than a dot. There are so many opportunities and so many needs around you right now that you can just about take your pick. Of course, you need to be wise and thoughtful, especially when it comes to doing God's work. Don't just rush into something because it seems like the right thing to do at the time. As you stay in the Word of God, talk to God through prayer, and listen to the Holy Spirit, your choices will be in line with God's will.

The People of God

You may be in the Word, your prayer life may be in excellent shape, and you may feel as though the Holy Spirit is prompting you to do something—but you're still not absolutely sure. Are you lacking faith? Not necessarily. More likely, you need a little more confirmation. That's where the wise counsel of other Christians comes into play. King Solomon, the wisest man who ever lived, didn't rely on his superior judgment and intellect alone. He sought out trusted advisers.

> *Plans go wrong for lack of advice; many counselors bring success* (Proverbs 15:22).

> *Though good advice lies deep within a person's heart, the wise will draw it out* (Proverbs 20:5).

> *As iron sharpens iron, a friend sharpens a friend* (Proverbs 27:17).

God doesn't expect you to make big decisions on your own. He has put people around you—your family, your friends, your pastor, your teachers, and even your boss—to give you advice and help you see things clearly. Ultimately the decision to follow God's will is yours, but remember that God uses others—especially other Christians—to help you know what His will is.

The Peace of God

Formerly, buying a car was followed by a seven-day "cooling-off" period, which was supposed to give you a chance to change your mind after you signed on the dotted line for that spiffy new Daewoo. The automobile manufacturers have stopped that practice (they were getting too many Daewoos back), but you can still incorporate a "cooling-off" period into your decision-making process. Especially when you make big decisions that have major consequences (like quitting your job so you can become a missionary), you need to step back and give God a chance to confirm your decision before you move ahead.

How does God do this? Besides the counsel of His Word, prayer, the Holy Spirit, and other people, He uses your inner organs to give you some strong clues (we're not kidding). If you are about to make a big decision (or you have already made it), and you find your stomach in knots, then you may want to go back through the decision-making principles to see if you missed anything. On the other hand, if your stomach feels fine and you have peace in your heart, then your decision is probably a good one. (Note: Don't get caught in the "ignorance is bliss" trap. Your peace is valid only if you have followed the other principles in your decision making.)

Growing in God

God has provided some amazing resources to help you know His will and make decisions, but nowhere does God guarantee that every decision or every circumstance will turn out the way you think it should. You will experience setbacks. You may even suffer. This doesn't mean you are out of the will of God. To the contrary, your negative experiences may be a part of God's plan for your life.

If you are drawing on God's resources and you are sure that you are doing what God wants you to do—and yet things aren't going well—then you can be sure that God is using your ordeal to help you grow as a Christian. Hang in there. Don't change course. God has promised to see you through your trials.

> *So, if you are suffering according to God's will, keep on doing what is right, and trust yourself to the God who made you, for he will never fail you* (1 Peter 4:19).

Two Traps to Avoid

God's will is always perfect, but sometimes in the process of trying to figure it out, you can trap yourself in some wrong thinking.

Subjectivity

One common trap is subjectivity. It's possible to become too subjective in the decision-making process. You're looking for the perfect confirmation to the problem or opportunity you are facing, and when you don't get it, you put off doing God's will because it just doesn't *feel* right. Paul Little advised, "We must not feel that every decision we make must have a subjective confirmation." Don't fall into the trap of standing still when God wants you to move. Too many well-intentioned Christians let their fear of the unknown (or worse, their fear of failure) stop them from doing what God wants them to do.

It's perfectly natural to become immobilized by the fear. That's why you need to call on the supernatural power of God to help you.

You need not be afraid of disaster or the destruction that comes upon the wicked, for the Lord is your security. He will keep your foot from being caught in a trap (Proverbs 3:25).

Passivity

Once you know what God wants you to do, don't be passive. Refusing to do God's will when you know what it is (especially if God has made it clear to you through His Word) is in direct disobedience to God.

Remember, it is sin to know what you ought to do and then not do it (James 4:17).

God wants nothing more than for you to follow Him by following His will. He wants you to follow the principles He has provided, but He won't force you. As the ultimate guide, God will come alongside you and show you which way to go. If you stand still, He won't drag you. If you veer off the path, He won't snag you. God is pointing the way, and it's up to you to move forward, making wise choices along the way.

What's That Again?

1. There are three things you can do to keep your decisions in the context of God's will: commit to do the will of God, see things from God's perspective, and let God work in you.

2. God may not reveal His will when you *think* you need it, but He will show you when He *knows* you need it.

3. God has given you the resources you need to make wise decisions in the context of His will for your life. These are the Word of God, talking with God, the Spirit of God, the work of God, the people of God, the peace of God, and growing in God.

4. Avoid the traps of subjectivity and passivity.

Dig Deeper

- *The Mystery of God's Will* by Charles R. Swindoll. According to Swindoll, God's will is not so much a destination as much as it is a journey.

- *How to Know the Will of God* by Russ Johnston. Another little booklet with a big message.

- *Real Life to the Extreme* by Bruce & Stan. The seven resources we list in this chapter were taken from this book we wrote about making choices that matter. We recommend it (even if we do say so ourselves).

Moving On

We hope this book on finding God's will has helped you better understand what God wants for you. As you have just read, there are lots of things you can do to discover God's will for today, tomorrow, and the rest of your life. But don't think for a minute that God is leaving everything up to you. "For God is working in you, giving you the desire to obey him and the power to do what pleases him" (Philippians 2:13).

This should give you tremendous confidence. As you make your choices and move forward, God is working in you and through you to accomplish His will in your life.

Other Books by the Guys

Bruce and Stan would enjoy hearing from you. (If you've got something nice to say, then don't hold back. If you have a criticism, then be gentle.) The best way to contact them is:

E-mail: **guide@bruceandstan.com**

Snail mail: Bruce & Stan
P.O. Box 25565
Fresno, CA 93729-5565

You can learn more than you ever wanted to know about Bruce and Stan by visiting their Web site: **www.bruceandstan.com**